This is an expression of love both verbal and visual.

I wrote the poems and then asked my good friend
Alex Gotfryd to interpret them visually.

The result is the sixteen page picture poem.

Write your own lines. And for the poetry,
draw your own pictures.

This book was designed by Herb Lubalin.

Lois Wyse
1979

Love Poems for a Rainy Day
by Lois Wyse

Love

Garret Press

Published by The Garret Press, 3126 Bremerton Road, Pepper Pike, Ohio. First printing 1979. Copyright ©1978, 1979 by Lois Wyse. All rights reserved ISBN 0-933628-11-0. Library of Congress catalog card number: 79-83527. Printed in the United States of America.

For a love that lasts.

Contents

Hello Sunshine, **1** Dr. Thinkgood, **2** The Opportunity for Love, **4** Single Woman, **5** Lesson, **6** Keeping Time, **7** The Other Woman, **8** One, Two., **10** Hearth-to-Hearth, **11** Trust Me, **12** A Good Love Works Because A Good Love Works, **13** Divorced Woman, **14** Equal Rights, **16** Color Photography, **17-32** Honestly, **33** Last Words, **34** Social Commentary, **35** The Cocktail Party, **36** All Aboard, **37** Married Woman, **38** I Knew Her When She Was A Brunette, **40** The Fidelity Gap, **41** Understanding, **42** Human Sexual Response, etc., **43** Sometimes Imperfect, Often Impossible, **44** The Twentieth Century Man, **45** The Widow, **46** Need, **48** Up the Up Escalator, **49** The Perfect Child, **50** This and That, **52**

Hello Sunshine

It rained last night,
That warm-washed rain of summertime
And other times
When you and love were here.

Did it rain on your life, too, last night?
And if it did
Were you awake to hear
And to remember
All the times that we held close
As another storm blew past?

I must tell you something, dear.
I no longer am afraid of rain,
For now I know
That no love but the one
That outlasts wet and weary times
Can be
The sunshine love of life.

Dr. Thinkgood

At a dinner party the other evening
I was seated next to a surgeon.
We dissected wines and politics
And finally we got around to women.
I know about the man/woman thing, he said.
        (Everybody does, Doctor).
But I really know.
I had to get married twice to find out.
The first time
I was married to a woman
Who said she would have loved me more
If my politics were different.

Now I am married to a woman
Who doesn't even know my politics.

She just gets pleasure out of me.
She loves loving me.
Isn't that simple?

Sometimes I reach out and touch her
Just because it makes me feel good.
A good marriage is simply feeling good.
It is pleasing yourself.
It really doesn't have a thing to do with
Politics or religion or who makes the bed.
My first wife?
Well, she married a man who is so conservative
He makes dull old me look like a card-carrying radical.

But you know something?
I don't think my first wife even sees the difference.
I realize now that it wasn't my politics she didn't love.
It was me.
And when you get to the point in life
When you know you're not right for someone
. .and not just that someone is not right for you. .
Well, then you've really grown up.

And you have the hurt to prove it.

The Opportunity for Love

A small brown wren she
Who said, "I never had
The opportunity for love."

Ah, little bird,
It is not
Opportunity
That creates love.

It is
Imagination.

Single Woman

Don't feel sorry for me.
In lots of ways
I like
The singleness of me.

I like
Watching TV,
Reading good books,
Washing my hair at 4 AM,
Playing any music I want
   ...and getting the whole bed.

I hate
Eating alone in restaurants,
Buying one ticket for the movies,
Going to bridal showers,
Listening to my mother
   ("Why isn't he good enough?"
     "You ought to see the nice man she married.")
   ...and Sunday.

I hope
Somewhere around the corner
I will find someone
Who will let me
Hold on to all I like,
Get rid of all I hate,
And nourish the essential me.

What scares me
Is that I might go
From single to zero
In marriage.

5

Lesson

It is so painful
To learn when to love.
But it is even more painful
To learn when not to love.

Keeping Time

Nine days away.
You are nine days away.
Time. It m o v e s   s   o   s   l   o   w.

One day away.
You are one day away.
Time. Itdoesnotmove.

The Other Woman

For a woman who is supposed
To do a lot of loving,
I sometimes do
A lot of hating.

I hate me for being so involved with him.
I hate him for not being involved enough with me.
I hate them for needing him.
It's all so—oh, so unloving.
And I never meant it to be that way.

All I wanted was a little love,
And it certainly started innocently enough.
But on our way to finding love
We lost our innocence.

When things get really intense between us
We touch and listen to music,
And we are so close and so much a part of each other
That we shut out all the rest of the world,
And he promises that some way we are going to live together,
And I cry and ask when.
And he holds me close and says, "Someday."

Someday I can go to his business dinners,
And someday those tickets I order for the theater will be for us,
Not for them.
Someday I'll be able to call him in the middle of the day,
And he'll drop everything to find out what's bothering me.
The way it is now I can't afford to tell him what's bothering me
Because he loves the no bother of me.
No stopped sinks in our relationship.
He adores the reality of our unreality.
But someday. . .
Someday, he says.

I don't know what will happen
If I tell him we're through.
I'm not sure I'm strong enough
To eat alone every night,
And I'm not sure I'm brave enough
To get into a bed that's cold on both sides.

And as much as I love
Meeting him at five
And dread
His leaving me at seven,
What would I do without those two hours?

What do I want?
Part-time Charlie
Or full-time, empty me?

I wish I knew what to do.

How do you know when
You want to change your life
And upset a clutch of people
In order to make yourself happy?

When do you decide
You have the right to decide?

More important. . .
When does he?

One, Two.

Single people
Are lonely and unhappy
Much of the time.

Just like
Married people.

Hearth-to-Hearth

So there you are.
Tired by the long distance run of now.
And here I am.
Tired by the pop pop pops of today.
And yet we know
That when we touch
You will forget the run
And all my little pops will slowly sputter
In the first quiet stirring
Of a rekindled love.

Trust Me

Here we are again.
You on one side of the bed,
I on the other.

You tightly bound by skepticism.
I freed by trust.

Know something, love?
I'd rather be me.

Maybe trusting someone too much
Causes pain tomorrow...
But, oh, what a nice today.

A Good Love Works
Because A Good Love Works

There really is no pattern
To a love that works.
Do her neuroses
Fit his psychoses?
Does his spaghetti
Match her sauce?
Don't ask me, my dear.

All I know for sure
Is that our love still works
So long as you can tell me
We are going to have two whole days together
  . . . and I am glad.

Divorced Woman

I'm getting a divorce.
Now maybe that news doesn't knock you out,
But it's tearing me up in little pieces.

To begin,
I always thought
Divorce, like marriage,
Was a private affair.
Well, it's not.
When you get a divorce
It's not just you and him.
It's his family and yours,
Friends, the people you work with, neighbors.
Hell, even the dry cleaner has an opinion.

In the beginning my friends came to see me.
It was like making a condolence call.
Everybody was looking around for the body,
But he had taken his body
To Palm Springs.

One friend told me
...After all, who but a dear friend would tell you...
That the story around town
Was that my husband
Was in love with another woman.

Another said she'd heard
I had a boy friend.
Oh my God, what a deadly expression.
A boy friend at my age.
Couldn't it at least be a lover?

One friend called to say
She didn't know how she and her husband
Would manage without us.
Her husband called and said the same thing.
Are we supposed to be the glue
For a lot of unstuck marriages?

Another friend said
She took tranquilizers and went to bed for two days.
And after a week of informing people,
I got to the point
Where I couldn't tell anyone
Because I couldn't stand seeing
The hurt on their faces.

What nobody realized was that
Underneath all that talk of
Alimony, custody and child support,
That beneath the surface of sympathetic clucking
There was a very scared woman
Who was falling apart.

Me.

Equal Rights

See that man? my friend inquired.
His wife left him two years ago,
And he still has not recovered.

I shook my head in disbelief.
You mean men hurt as much as women do?

Honestly

You do not lie.
Oh no, you never lie.
Instead you cut
A careful pattern
And refit the truth
To fit your reasons.

You know, my dear,
There are times
I would prefer
A good, fat lie.

Last Words

Look, she said,
I just can't stand it
One minute longer.

        What?

I'm leaving.
I'm getting out.
I'm through.

        Because just once
        I had an affair?

Yes.

        But I don't love her.
        I swear.
        All I did was
        Go to bed with her.
        I do not love her.

That, my dear,
Is why I am leaving.
You see, I could have stayed
If you had loved her.

Social Commentary

Ridiculous, the dinner guests agreed.
Absolutely ridiculous
That a woman her age
Be so—well, so obviously—involved
With a man his age.

> "Besides, he's not even good-looking."
> "Of course, she isn't either."
> "But at least he's young."

Ah, my charming dinner guests
(Who count calories and birthdays,
Who measure men in dollars and in dividends)
Can you last remember
When anyone of any age
Seemed so—well, so obviously—involved
With you?

The Cocktail Party

Are you married, he asked.
Yes, she answered,
But I'm not fanatic about it.

Of course not.
Nobody today is fanatic about marriage.
Nowadays we are fanatic about
Upstairs/Downstairs
Gold bullion
And new apartments.

After all,
Over a glass of white wine and two canapes
Who wants to hear it for something your mother likes?

All Aboard

There is a small commuter train
That runs a fast and silent track
Between your mind and mine.

Somedays the train is overcrowded,
A lot of hangers-on,
Back to the bar car.

Then there are times when you may be
The solitary passenger
On the long and bumpy road to me.

And we both know the dreary days
When it would be
So easy to turn back.

Yet each time you have chugged on.
And although I do not always seem a grateful woman,
I really am so glad you bought
That one-way ticket a long, long time ago.

Married Woman

I come from the old time
When marriage was the answer
To this, the new time,
When marriage is the question.

And, like many women in my world these days,
I wonder if there is something wrong with me
To want marriage
And not The Other Possibilities.

Possibilities that do not require
Commitment,
Hope
Or faith.

But what is life without the faith
That precedes commitment?
Is the road worth taking without the hope
That sustains despair?

A married woman learns
To rule the world
In the confines of her home,
In the shadows of her hope,
In the fire of her faith,
In commitment to her love.

Married?
Why am I married?

Caught in the sea
Of changing linens and changing attitudes,
Supervising the household of pepper mills and salt shakers?

Why am I married?

Because beyond the shifting winds and low-lying clouds
I have yet to see a sign
That anything but marriage
Is the future of mankind.

I Knew Her When She Was A Brunette

I have been married
A very long time.

And in that time
My husband
Has had three wives—
All of them
Me.

The Fidelity Gap

So many sounds to lure me
So many views to tempt me
So, for a moment, I may stray.

But it would not be natural
If I never heard the music
Of other violins
And never saw the view
Beyond the second story.

Understanding

I do not know the words
Of that small song in my heart,
But somehow, my dear,
I think you do.

Human Sexual Response, etc.

You can take all the how-to books
And all the why-not literature,
Give them to all the lab technicians
And all the slide rule specialists,

And not one of them will ever know
The measure of trust
That goes into love –
Which is the only human response
No one has learned to measure.

Sometimes Imperfect, Often Impossible

You are
Sometimes imperfect,
Often impossible

And still I love you

Because, my sweet, you are
The only man in the world
Who makes me feel
At home in the world

Even though I am
Sometimes imperfect,
Often impossible

The Twentieth Century Man

J. D. is terribly rich
(Of course)
Except for
His guilt-edged insecurities.

The Widow

In the beginning
I would look at my watch and say,
"Yesterday he was here."

It has been a long time now since
I looked at my watch.
It has been so long
I do not even look at the calendar.

But in the beginning
People listened to each detail
As if listening confirmed their mortality.
They were still here at the end of the story.
I guess fresh grief is like fresh milk.
We consume it quickly before it sours.

But grief cannot be worn
Season after season
Like a string of pearls.

Mourning becomes an embarrassment
To those who watch
The seasons of our sorrow.

A well-behaved widow
Does not cry.
(Me? Cry? Just because
I am lonesome for
The only man I ever loved)

A good widow
Gets on with life
(I brush my teeth and do not beat
My hands against the wall. I never look up
From my needlepoint and ask, "Why?")

A proper widow
Knows her place.
(Of course, I understand that
You will invite me to the next party. . .
The one with women only)

A thoughtful widow
Makes no demands on children,
(I smile and tell them yes, go ahead.
I know you have your own life. I do not say
Once I had a life–)

I think now as I lie here in the dark
Of all the things we meant to do.
Alone they are nothing. But who wants
To listen to the solo song of widowhood?

No one but another widow, for she
Is the only one who knows the bitter truth.
It never gets better.
It only gets ordinary.

Need

The problem for those who love
Is those we love.
They are afraid
We need them too much.

And so we do.

But until we can stop our need
Long enough
To stop our love
They will never know
How much they need us.

And so they do.

Up the Up Escalator

She leaned and looked back
At the lanky form that lounged
Near the last step of the escalator.
Don't worry, she called,
The bitter taste won't last.

How do you know? he asked.

It never does with yogurt, she replied.

Do I dare tell her that it does
With almost everything else?

The Perfect Child

She was the perfect child
Who marched to her mother's beat
A beat in time replaced by
Teacher, husband, children, job.

> Rat-a-tat
> Let's hear it for
> The four-square
> Ordered life.

Just a minute.
Who ordered life?
Not she.

She ordered beauty, dignity and reason.
(After all, she was the perfect child)
But what she got was life.

> She ordered out of
> Column A
> And what she got was
> Ratatouille.

She reordered the disorder

> "Four wallet size
> And enlarge two."

But somehow the enlargement
Was not as big as life itself
And she still could not find herself
On the fine-tuned screen.

What ever became of the order
Of her early four-square life?

> Is it behind doors that do not open?
> Flying out of windows that do not shut?

She speaks if anyone should ask:

> She says that she is out.
> Out of step,
> Out of sorts,
> And, in her perpetual confusion,
> She is definitely
> Out of order.

And her mother nods and says,
Ah, she was the perfect child.

This and That

It rained again today,
And when I left
Coated, booted and umbrella-d,
People said,
You mean you're going out in that?

What they did not know,
My love, is
I went out in that
For this.

Books by Lois Wyse:Poetry/Love Poems for the Very Married/Are You Sure You Love Me?/I Love You Better Now/Wet Paint and Other Signs of Love **Novels**/The Rosemary Touch/Kiss, Inc./Far from Innocence

Designed by
Herb Lubalin and Michael Aron
Photography by Alex Gotfryd